MEET THE ELEPHANT!

Written by Keith Faulkner
Illustrated by Robert Morton

GT PUBLISHING

Copyright © 1996 Brainwaves Limited.
All rights reserved. No part of this book may be used or reproduced
in any manner whatsoever without written permission from the publisher.

This edition published by GT Publishing Corporation.

For information address GT Publishing Corporation, 16 East 40th Street,
New York, New York 10016.

ISBN: 1-57719-092-0

Printed in Singapore.

Meet the Elephant

The elephant is the largest land mammal living on the planet today. Let's take a closer look at this powerful creature.

The African Elephant

The African elephant is native to the grassy plains of Africa south of the Sahara Desert.

The Indian Elephant

The Indian elephant is found in India, Sri Lanka, Sumatra and other parts of Southeast Asia.

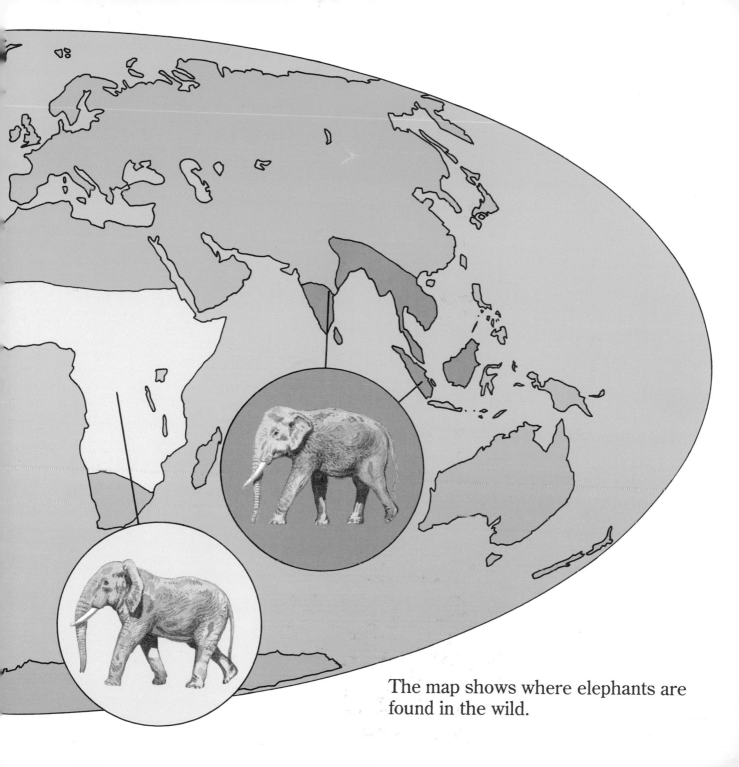

The map shows where elephants are found in the wild.

The Torso

A male, or bull, African elephant measures up to eleven feet tall from the ground to its shoulders, and can weigh more than six tons. The male Indian elephant is smaller, averaging nine feet tall at the shoulder and weighing three and one-half tons. The elephant in the picture is carrying a *howdah* and has been painted and decorated for ceremonial purposes.

Turn to the back of the book and push out the torso piece.

The Legs

The elephant needs very strong legs to support such a massive torso. Its huge legs end in flat feet which help to prevent the elephant from sinking into soft ground. The elephant can use its powerful legs to reach speeds up to 30 miles an hour, but it cannot jump at all.

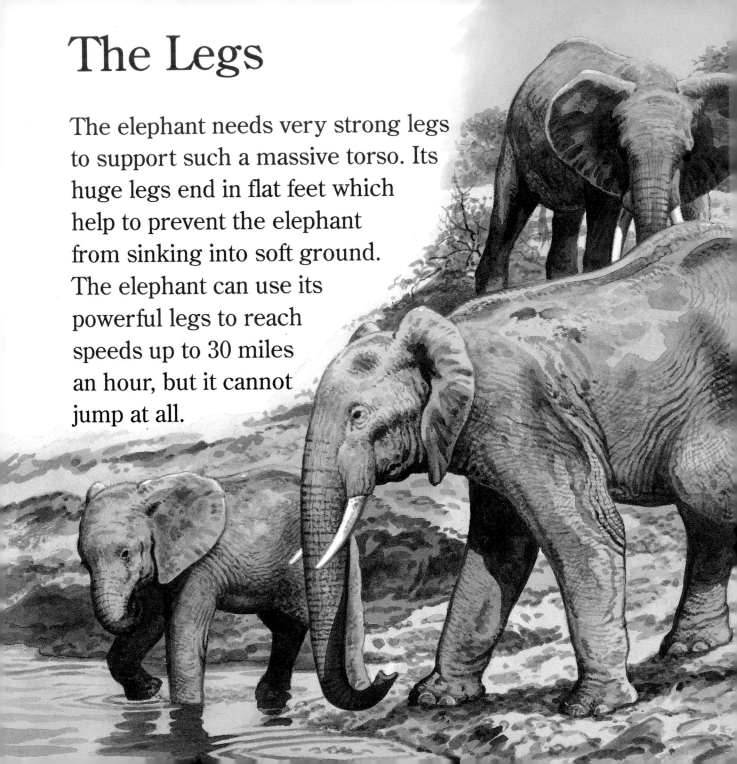

Elephants' feet are covered with very thick skin, but even so, Hannibal had leather boots made for them when he used elephants to cross the Alps to attack the Romans in 218 BC.

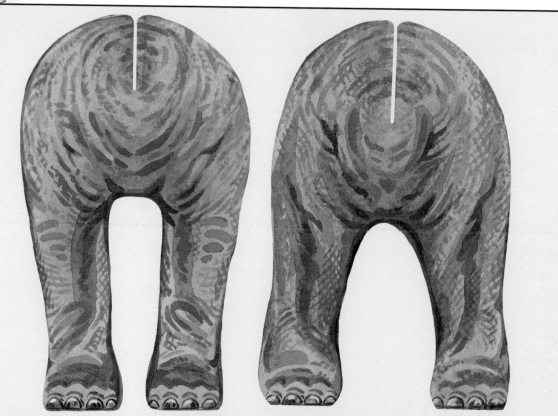

Find the front and back leg pieces and attach them to the torso.

The Ears

The elephant's large ears help keep the animal cool in hot weather. The ears work like giant fans when the elephant flaps them to create a cooling breeze.

But flapping ears can also be a sign of anger. An adult elephant flapping its ears will scare even a lion.

Find the ears and put them on the head.

The Trunk

An elephant's trunk is a very useful thing. It can pick up something as small as a peanut with the finger-like tip, or pull down strong branches. When an elephant wants a shower it can suck water into its trunk to squirt over its back.

Now find the elephant's trunk piece and slot it into place.

The Tusks

The elephant's large ivory tusks are actually teeth that grow out from the mouth. A male African elephant's tusks can reach more than ten feet in length and weigh over two hundred pounds each.